DEXTERITY EXER

for the Electric Bass

By Rob Chiarelli

Photo by Michael Becker Photography

Cover art by Levin Pfeufer

Cherry Lane Music Company
Educational Director/Project Supervisor: Susan Poliniak
Director of Publications: Mark Phillips
Publications Coordinator: Rebecca Skidmore

ISBN 978-1-60378-195-4

Visit our website at www.cherrylaneprint.com

CONTENTS

ABOUT THE AUTHOR

Rob Chiarelli is a record producer and mix engineer based in Los Angeles, CA. Widely recognized as a producer on Will Smith's *Men in Black II* album, Chiarelli's work appears on numerous gold and platinum records as well as several motion picture soundtracks, including seven Grammy winners. As a bassist, Chiarelli's work can be heard on many of the same recordings he has produced and mixed.

Chiarelli's clients include pop superstars Will Smith, Mary Mary, The New Boyz, Christina Aguilera, and Janet Jackson; television stars Hilary Duff, Paula Abdul, the Jonas Brothers, Big Time Rush, and Miranda Cosgrove; country superstar LeAnn Rimes; the iconic Ray Charles and Johnny Mathis; jazz greats Keiko Matsui and Everette Harp; world music icon Waldemar Bastos; and rock superstar Josh Todd (Buckcherry).

A Boston-area native, Chiarelli began studying music at an early age and quickly excelled at both drums and electric bass guitar. He received early recognition of his talent, including several honors from the National Association of Jazz Educators and scholarships to the University Of Miami for both Jazz Bass and Orchestral Percussion.

After a brief tour with his own band, Chiarelli turned his attention to producing/engineering and relocated to Los Angeles in 1989. That same year he mixed chart-topping hits for Club Nouveau and the Calloway Brothers. A succession of hits followed with artists such as Janet Jackson, Ray Charles, Keiko Matsui, Coolio, Ice Cube, Queen Latifah, Adina Howard, Jade, the Temptations, En Vogue, Chuckii Booker, and many others. By 1997, in a joint venture with Red Ant/BMG, Chiarelli was running his own record label and working with every major record company in the United States, Europe, and Japan.

Now a 20-year veteran of the industry, Rob Chiarelli is a sought-after mixer, producer, and musician who continues to appreciate working with great artists. He enjoys regular speaking engagements at the University of Illinois, the Berklee College of Music, the International Digital Rights Foundation, California Lawyers for the Arts, and TAXI, among others. Chiarelli has also appeared in a number of highly respected industry publications including *Recording Magazine, EQ Magazine, A&R, Music Connection, Mix Magazine,* and *Pro Sound News.*

When he's not in the studio, Chiarelli spends his time coaching baseball and teaching his kids to play the same classic rock tunes he enjoyed in his own youth.

DEDICATION

This work is dedicated to my devoted parents, Evelyn and Charles Chiarelli, and to my brother Mike who has always been my hero and inspiration.

ACKNOWLEDGMENTS

This book was inspired by the teachings of Tom Dumas, Walter Tokarczyk, Tom Ferrante, Emmanuel Gatewood, Don Coffman, Vince Maggio, Tim Goodwin, and all of the brilliant teachers and musicians with whom I have studied and worked during my life. All of them gave generously to their students, to music, and to art.

This book would not be possible without the contributions of my wife Theresa, my son Robert, and my daughter Angela. Thanks to them for giving so selflessly and for their constant encouragement, love, and support.

Thanks to John Stix and Susan Poliniak at Cherry Lane for their generous support and assistance in bringing this volume to print.

Special thanks to Stephen N. Limbaugh, Michael Becker, Christine Wu, Heather Wagner, Nate Highfield, and Reggie Hamilton.

INTRODUCTION

This book contains a series of exercises created to develop technical mastery of the electric bass. It has been designed to give players of all levels a set of practical routines that are both meaningful and easily understood. These exercises can help to stretch the fingers and relax the hand. With repeated practice and proper execution, these exercises can build strength, endurance, and the proper technique necessary to communicate a wide range of musical ideas.

PHILOSOPHY

Some of the exercises contained in this book are designed to strengthen both the fingers and the hand. Others are designed to help the player relax and build technique. Still others are designed to stretch the fingers and allow ease of movement when shifting along the neck. Although the exercises here can broaden each player's technical foundation, it is important to recognize that *technique is no substitute for musicianship*. It is the goal of this book to help the player overcome any technical limitations clearing the path for true musical expression.

HOW TO USE THIS BOOK

Most of the exercises contained in this volume are short and have simple patterns that can be repeated. The exercises become progressively more difficult throughout the book. Although they are notated in 2nd position—fretted with the index finger at the 2nd fret, the middle finger at the 3rd fret, the ring finger at the 4th fret, and the pinky at the 5th—it is important to play each of these exercises in all possible positions. This is especially true for the fretless bass player.

This book also may be used for lessons of a few exercises per week, or even as a weekly study. Some bassists may also wish to "pick and choose" specific exercises based on their personal needs and preferences.

PRACTICING

The purpose of this book is to help you play dramatically better *without* tension. Always take care to keep your hands, arms, and neck as relaxed as possible. Take breaks as often as needed, and never force your muscles. Make a daily effort to stretch your wrists, arms, and neck. Keep in mind that playing the electric bass is an athletic endeavor.

Begin each exercise slowly. Increase the tempo of each exercise gradually, and only when you can perform the exercise cleanly without compromising the rhythm or tone at a slower tempo. Attack each note decisively and repeat each routine. Mastering each exercise at a slow tempo is the most important element for achieving maximum benefit from this system. Furthermore, true mastery of any fast tempo depends on this same concept. As you gradually increase the tempo, it is crucial that you periodically return to slower tempos as well. This is the foundation of any advanced level of dexterity: While it may be tempting to play as fast as possible, it is important to remember that practicing at both slow and fast tempos is equally important.

KEEP IN MIND

- Consistency is the key to mastery. Make these exercises a regular part of your practice routine.

- When you approach an exercise for the first time, practice it with your metronome set to 60 beats per minute. Increase the tempo gradually and return to slower tempos periodically.

- Take care to relax your hands. Take breaks as often as needed.

- These exercises may be practiced with straight eighth notes or in a swing feel.

- In addition to playing each exercise as written, it is also recommended that you try playing with two (or three or four) attacks per notated note (e.g., subdivide each eighth note into 16th, 32nd, or 64th notes, and attack each note separately)

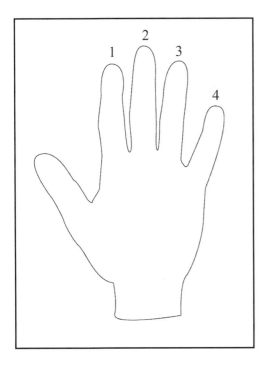

NOTATION

All of the exercises are notated in second position with proper fingerings (as 1, 2, 3, and 4).

There is also a tab staff below each exercise showing the corresponding string and fret for each note.

NUMBER 1

Begin with the 1st finger on the G string.

Begin with the 1st finger on the D string.

Begin with the 1st finger on the A string.

Begin with the 1st finger on the E string.

This study combines the exercises above.

NUMBER 2

Begin with the 4th finger on the G string.

Begin with the 4th finger on the D string.

Begin with the 4th finger on the A string.

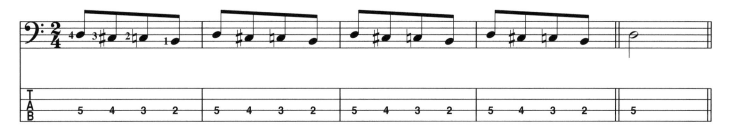

Begin with the 4th finger on the E string.

This study combines the exercises above.

NUMBER 3

Begin with the 3rd finger on the G string.

Begin with the 3rd finger on the D string.

Begin with the 3rd finger on the A string.

Begin with the 3rd finger on the E string.

This study combines the exercises above.

NUMBER 4

Begin with the 4th finger on the G string.

Begin with the 4th finger on the D string.

Begin with the 4th finger on the A string.

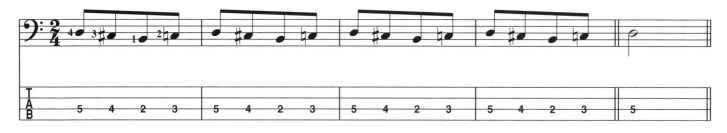

Begin with the 4th finger on the E string.

This study combines the exercises above.

NUMBER 5

Begin with the 1st finger on the G string.

Begin with the 1st finger on the D string.

Begin with the 1st finger on the A string.

Begin with the 1st finger on the E string.

This study combines the exercises above.

NUMBER 6

Begin with the 2nd finger on the G string.

Begin with the 2nd finger on the D string.

Begin with the 2nd finger on the A string.

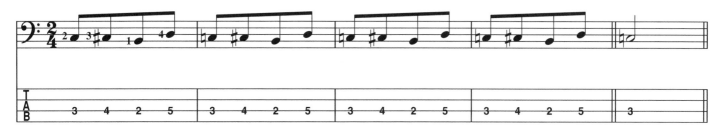

Begin with the 2nd finger on the E string.

This study combines the exercises above.

Begin with the 4th finger on the G string.

Begin with the 4th finger on the D string.

Begin with the 4th finger on the A string.

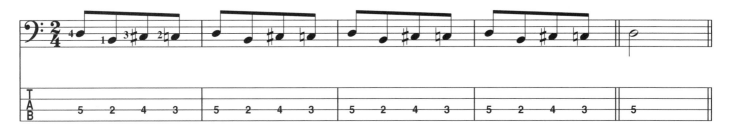

Begin with the 4th finger on the E string.

This study combines the exercises above.

NUMBER 8

Begin with the 3rd finger on the D string.

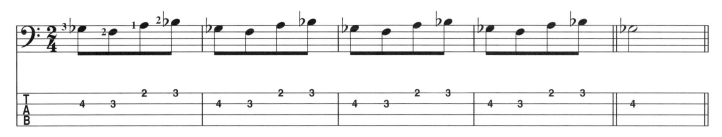

Begin with the 3rd finger on the A string.

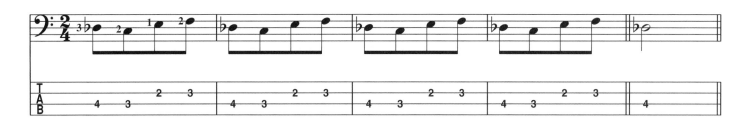

Begin with the 3rd finger on the E string.

This study combines the exercises above.

NUMBER 9

Begin with the 4th finger on the D string.

Begin with the 4th finger on the A string.

Begin with the 4th finger on the E string.

This study combines the exercises above.

NUMBER 10

Begin with the 2nd finger on the D string.

Begin with the 2nd finger on the A string.

Begin with the 2nd finger on the E string.

This study combines the exercises above.

NUMBER 11

Begin with the 3rd finger on the D string.

Begin with the 3rd finger on the A string.

Begin with the 3rd finger on the E string.

This study combines the exercises above.

16

NUMBER 12

Begin with the 1st finger on the D string.

Begin with the 1st finger on the A string.

Begin with the 1st finger on the E string.

This study combines the exercises above.

NUMBER 13

Begin with the 4th finger on the G string.

Begin with the 4th finger on the D string.

Begin with the 4th finger on the A string.

This study combines the exercises above.

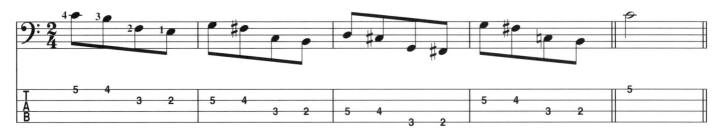

NUMBER 14

Begin with the 3rd finger on the G string.

Begin with the 3rd finger on the D string.

Begin with the 3rd finger on the A string.

This study follows the pattern of the exercises above.

NUMBER 15

Begin with the 2nd finger on the E string.

Begin with the 2nd finger on the A string.

Begin with the 2nd finger on the D string.

This study combines the exercises above.

NUMBER 16

Begin with the 1st finger on the E string.

Begin with the 1st finger on the A string.

Begin with the 1st finger on the D string.

This study combines the exercises above.

NUMBER 17

Begin with the 3rd finger on the G string.

Begin with the 3rd finger on the D string.

Begin with the 3rd finger on the A string.

This study combines the exercises above.

NUMBER 18

Begin with the 4th finger on the G string.

Begin with the 4th finger on the D string.

Begin with the 4th finger on the A string.

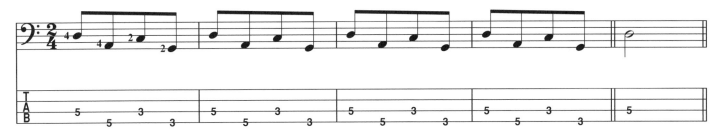

This study combines the exercises above.

NUMBER 19

Begin with the 2nd finger on the G string.

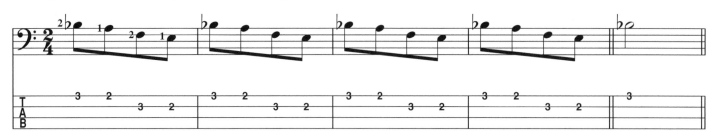

Begin with the 2nd finger on the D string.

Begin with the 2nd finger on the A string.

This study follows the pattern of the exercises above.

NUMBER 20

Begin with the 3rd finger on the G string.

Begin with the 3rd finger on the D string.

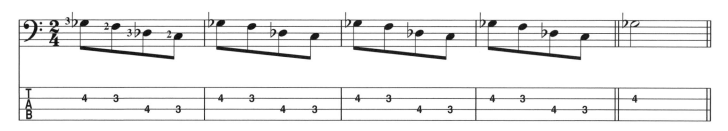

Begin with the 3rd finger on the A string.

This study follows the pattern of the exercises above.

NUMBER 21

Begin with the 4th finger on the G string.

Begin with the 4th finger on the D string.

Begin with the 4th finger on the A string.

This study follows the pattern of the exercises above.

NUMBER 22

Begin with the 1st finger on the D string.

Begin with the 1st finger on the A string.

Begin with the 1st finger on the E string.

This study follows the pattern of the exercises above.

NUMBER 23

Begin with the 2nd finger on the D string.

Begin with the 2nd finger on the A string.

Begin with the 2nd finger on the E string.

This study follows the pattern of the exercises above.

Begin with the 3rd finger on the D string.

Begin with the 3rd finger on the A string.

Begin with the 3rd finger on the E string.

This study follows the pattern of the exercises above.

NUMBER 25

Begin with the 2nd finger on the G string.

Begin with the 3rd finger on the G string.

Begin with the 4th finger on the G string.

This study combines the exercises above.

NUMBER 26

Begin with the 1st finger on the E string.

Begin with the 2nd finger on the E string.

Begin with the 3rd finger on the E string.

This study combines the exercises above.

NUMBER 27

Begin with the 1st finger on the G string.

Begin with the 1st finger on the D string.

Begin with the 1st finger on the A string.

This study combines the exercises above.

NUMBER 28

Begin with the 3rd finger on the D string.

Begin with the 3rd finger on the A string.

Begin with the 3rd finger on the E string.

This study combines the exercises above.

NUMBER 29

Begin with the 4th finger on the D string.

Begin with the 4th finger on the A string.

Begin with the 4th finger on the E string.

This study combines the exercises above.

NUMBER 30

Begin with the 2nd finger on the D string.

Begin with the 2nd finger on the A string.

Begin with the 2nd finger on the E string.

This study combines the exercises above.

NUMBER 31

Begin with the 3rd finger on the G string.

Begin with the 3rd finger on the D string.

Begin with the 3rd finger on the A string.

This study combines the exercises above.

NUMBER 32

Begin with the 3rd finger on the D string.

Begin with the 3rd finger on the A string.

Begin with the 3rd finger on the E string.

This study combines the exercises above.

NUMBER 33

Begin with the 4th finger on the G string.

Begin with the 4th finger on the D string.

Begin with the 4th finger on the A string.

This study combines the exercises above.

NUMBER 34

Begin with the 2nd finger on the G string.

Begin with the 2nd finger on the D string.

Begin with the 2nd finger on the A string.

This study combines the exercises above.

NUMBER 35

Begin with the 1st finger on the D string.

Begin with the 1st finger on the A string.

Begin with the 1st finger on the E string.

This study combines the exercises above.

NUMBER 36

Begin with the 1st finger on the E string.

Begin with the 1st finger on the A string.

Begin with the 1st finger on the D string.

Begin with the 1st finger on the G string.

This study combines the exercises above.

Begin with the 4th finger on the G string.

Begin with the 4th finger on the D string.

Begin with the 4th finger on the A string.

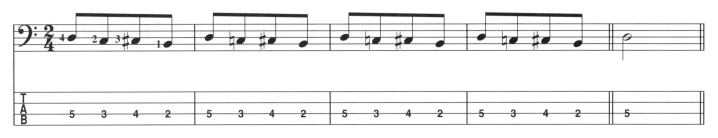

Begin with the 4th finger on the E string.

This study combines the exercises above.

NUMBER 38

Begin with the 1st finger on the G string.

Begin with the 4th finger on the E string.

This study combines the exercises above.

NUMBER 39

Begin with the 2nd finger on the E string.

Begin with the 3rd finger on the G string.

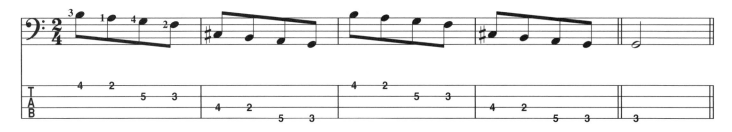

This study combines the exercises above.

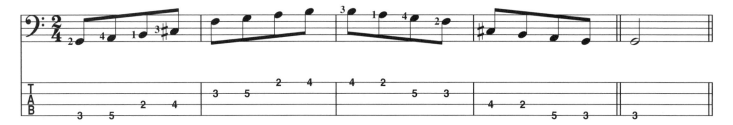

NUMBER 40

Begin with the 2nd finger on the E string.

Begin with the 2nd finger on the A string.

Begin with the 2nd finger on the D string.

This study follows the pattern of the exercises above.

NUMBER 41

Begin with the 4th finger on the E string.

Begin with the 4th finger on the A string.

Begin with the 4th finger on the D string.

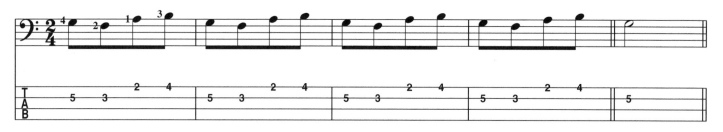

This study follows the pattern of the exercises above.

NUMBER 42

Begin with the 4th finger on the G string.

Begin with the 2nd finger on the E string.

This study combines the exercises above.

NUMBER 43

Begin with the 1st finger on the E string.

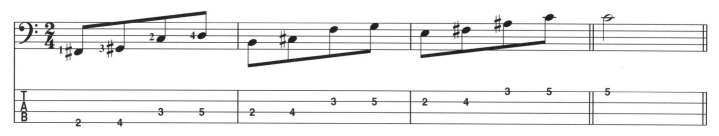

Begin with the 4th finger on the G string.

This study combines the exercises above.

NUMBER 44

Begin with the 1st finger on the E string.

Begin with the 4th finger on the G string.

This study combines the exercises above.

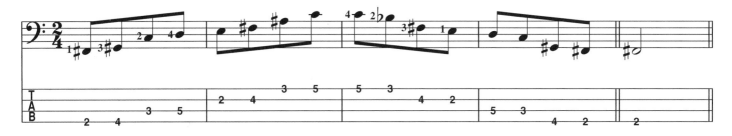

NUMBER 45

Begin with the 1st finger on the E string.

Begin with the 4th finger on the G string.

This study combines the exercises above.

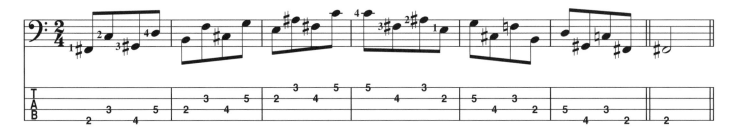

NUMBER 46

Begin with the 2nd finger on the E string.

Begin with the 3rd finger on the G string.

This study combines the exercises above.

NUMBER 47

Begin with the 1st finger on the E string.

Begin with the 1st finger on the A string.

Begin with the 1st finger on the D string.

This study combines the exercises above.

NUMBER 48

Begin with the 4th finger on the G string.

Begin with the 4th finger on the D string.

Begin with the 4th finger on the A string.

This study combines the exercises above.

Begin with the 1st finger on the E string.

Begin with the 1st finger on the A string.

Begin with the 1st finger on the D string.

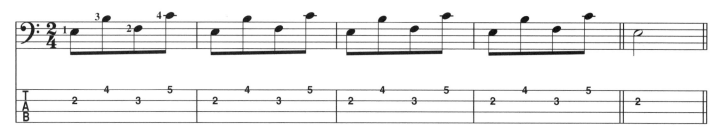

This study combines the exercises above.

NUMBER 50

Begin with the 4th finger on the G string.

Begin with the 4th finger on the D string.

Begin with the 4th finger on the A string.

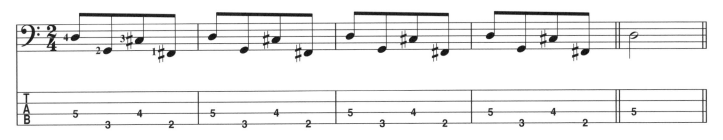

This study combines the exercises above.

NUMBER 51

Begin with the 1st finger on the E string.

Begin with the 1st finger on the A string.

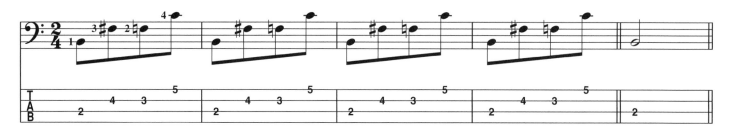

This study combines the exercises above.

Begin with the 4th finger on the G string.

Begin with the 4th finger on the D string.

This study combines the exercises above.

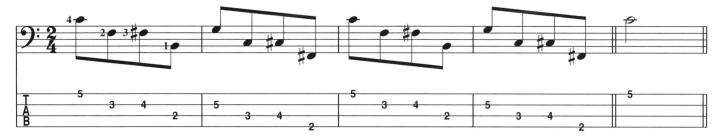

Begin with the 1st finger on the A string.

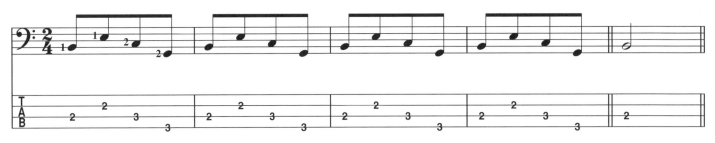

Begin with the 1st finger on the D string.

This study combines the exercises above.

NUMBER 54

Begin with the 2nd finger on the A string.

Begin with the 2nd finger on the D string.

This study combines the exercises above.

NUMBER 55

Begin with the 3rd finger on the A string.

Begin with the 3rd finger on the D string.

This study combines the exercises above.

NUMBER 56

Begin with the 1st finger on the A string.

Begin with the 3rd finger on the A string.

Begin with the 1st finger on the D string.

Begin with the 3rd finger on the D string.

This study combines the exercises above.

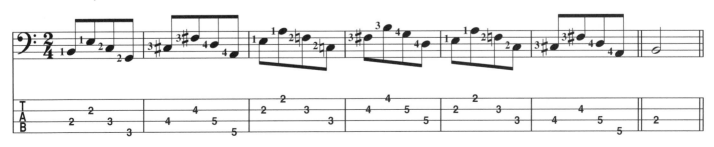

Begin with the 2nd finger on the D string.

Begin with the 2nd finger on the A string.

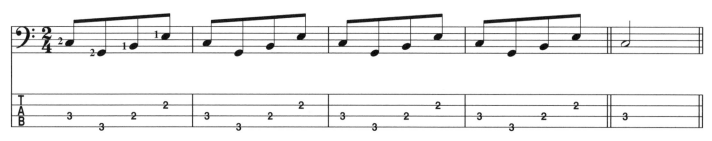

Begin with the 4th finger on the D string.

Begin with the 4th finger on the A string.

This study follows the pattern of the exercises above.

NUMBER 58

Begin with the 4th finger on the A string.

Begin with the 4th finger on the D string.

This study combines the exercises above.

NUMBER 59

Begin with the 3rd finger on the A string.

Begin with the 3rd finger on the D string.

This study combines the exercises above.

NUMBER 60

Begin with the 1st finger on the A string.

Begin with the 1st finger on the D string.

Begin with the 1st finger on the G string.

This study combines the exercises above.

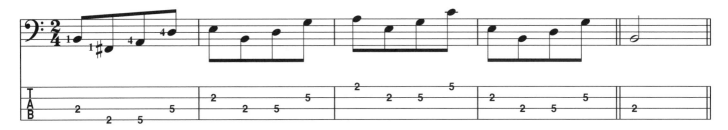

NUMBER 61

Begin with the 4th finger on the A string.

Begin with the 4th finger on the D string.

Begin with the 4th finger on the G string.

This study combines the exercises above.

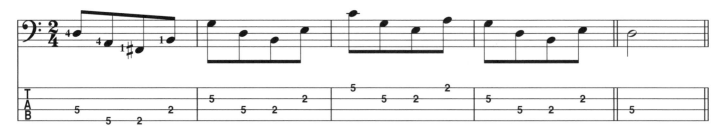

Begin with the 1st finger on the E string.

Begin with the 1st finger on the A string.

Begin with the 1st finger on the D string.

This study combines the exercises above.

Begin with the 4th finger on the E string.

Begin with the 4th finger on the A string.

Begin with the 4th finger on the D string.

This study combines the exercises above.

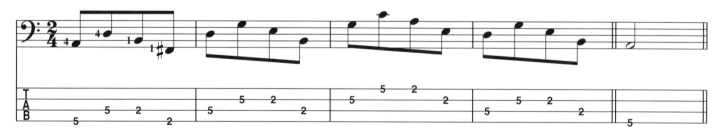

NUMBER 64

Begin with the 3rd finger on the A string.

Begin with the 3rd finger on the D string.

Begin with the 3rd finger on the G string.

This study combines the exercises above.

NUMBER 65

Begin with the 4th finger on the A string.

Begin with the 4th finger on the D string.

Begin with the 4th finger on the G string.

This study combines the exercises above.

NUMBER 66

Begin with the 1st finger on the G string.

Begin with the 1st finger on the D string.

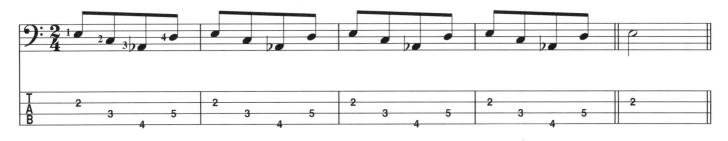

This study combines the exercises above.

NUMBER 67

Begin with the 4th finger on the G string.

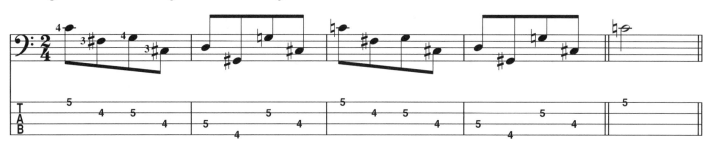

Begin with the 3rd finger on the G string.

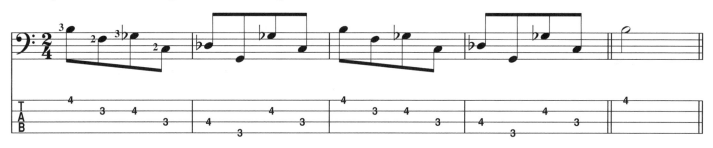

Begin with the 2nd finger on the G string.

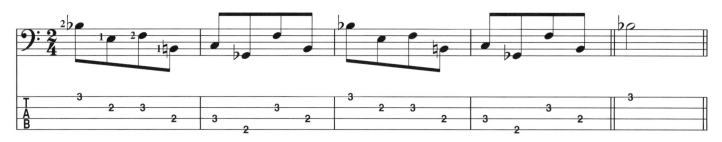

This study follows the pattern of the exercises above, but with a change of time signature.

NUMBER 68

Begin with the 3rd finger on the E string.

Begin with the 2nd finger on the E string.

Begin with the 1st finger on the E string.

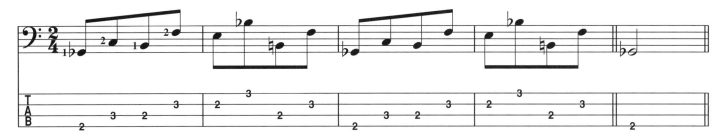

This study follows the pattern of the exercises above, but with a change of time signature.

NUMBER 69

Begin with the 3rd finger on the G string.

Begin with the 3rd finger on the D string.

Begin with the 3rd finger on the A string.

Begin with the 3rd finger on the E string.

This study combines the exercises above.

NUMBER 70

Begin with the 3rd finger on the G string.

Begin with the 3rd finger on the D string.

Begin with the 3rd finger on the A string.

This study combines the exercises above.

NUMBER 71

Begin with the 4th finger on the D string.

Begin with the 4th finger on the A string.

Begin with the 4th finger on the E string.

This study combines the exercises above.

NUMBER 72

Begin with the 4th finger on the G string.

Begin with the 3rd finger on the E string.

This study combines the exercises above.

NUMBER 73

Begin with the 3rd finger on the G string.

Begin with the 2nd finger on the E string.

This study combines the exercises above.

NUMBER 74

Begin with the 2nd finger on the G string.

Begin with the 1st finger on the E string.

This study combines the exercises above.

NUMBER 75

Begin with the 1st finger on the E string.

Begin with the 1st finger on the A string.

Begin with the 1st finger on the D string.

This study combines the exercises above.

NUMBER 76

Begin with the 4th finger on the G string.

Begin with the 4th finger on the D string.

Begin with the 4th finger on the A string.

This study combines the exercises above.

NUMBER 77

Begin with the 3rd finger on the D string.

Begin with the 3rd finger on the A string.

Begin with the 3rd finger on the E string.

This study combines the exercises above.

NUMBER 78

Begin with the 4th finger on the G string.

Begin with the 1st finger on the E string.

This study combines the exercises above.

NUMBER 79

Begin with the 1st finger on the E string.

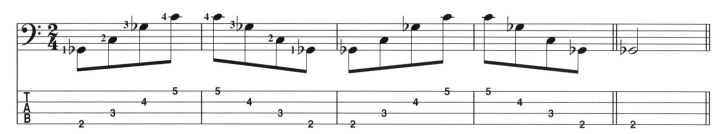

Begin with the 4th finger on the G string.

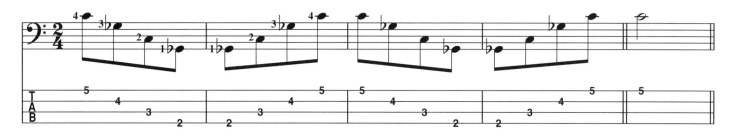

NUMBER 80

Begin with the 1st finger on the E string.

Begin with the 3rd finger on the E string.

Begin with the 2nd finger on the E string.

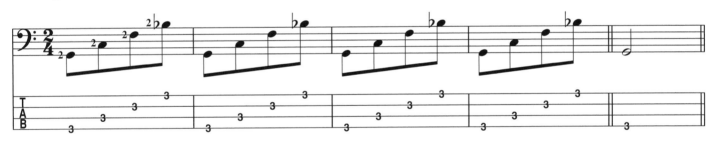

Begin with the 4th finger on the E string.

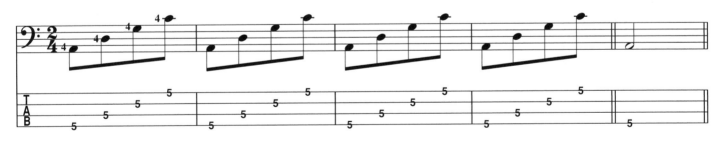

This study combines the exercises above.

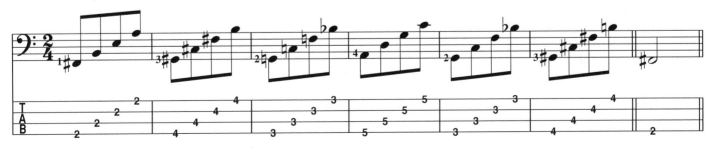

NUMBER 81

Begin with the 1st finger on the G string.

Begin with the 3rd finger on the G string.

Begin with the 2nd finger on the G string.

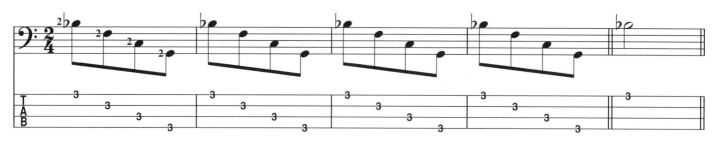

Begin with the 4th finger on the G string.

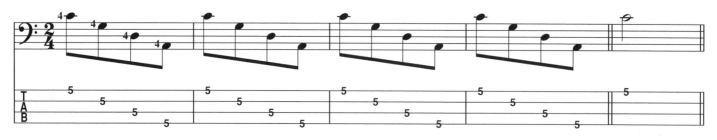

This study combines the exercises above.

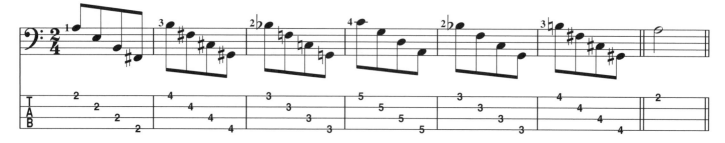

NUMBER 82

Begin with the 1st finger on the E string.

Begin with the 1st finger on the A string.

This study combines the exercises above.

NUMBER 83

Begin with the 4th finger on the D string.

Begin with the 4th finger on the G string.

This study combines the exercises above.

NUMBER 84

Begin with the 1st finger on the G string.

Begin with the 1st finger on the D string.

Begin with the 1st finger on the A string.

Begin with the 1st finger on the E string.

This study combines the exercises above.

NUMBER 85

Begin with the 1st finger on the G string.

Begin with the 1st finger on the D string.

Begin with the 1st finger on the A string.

This study combines the exercises above.

NUMBER 86

Begin with the 1st finger on the E string.

Begin with the 1st finger on the A string.

Begin with the 1st finger on the D string.

This study combines the exercises above.

NUMBER 87

Begin with the 4th finger on the G string.

Begin with the 3rd finger on the G string.

92

Begin with the 2nd finger on the G string.

This study combines the exercises above.

Begin with the 3rd finger on the G string.

Begin with the 3rd finger on the D string.

Begin with the 3rd finger on the A string.

This study combines the exercises above.

NUMBER 89

Begin with the 4th finger on the G string.

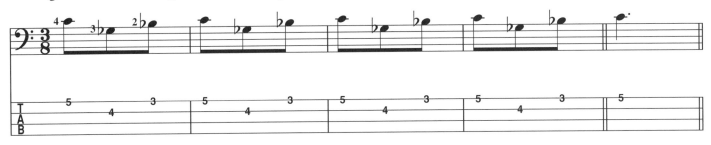

Begin with the 4th finger on the D string.

Begin with the 4th finger on the A string.

This study combines the exercises above.

Begin with the 2nd finger on the E string.

Begin with the 2nd finger on the A string.

Begin with the 2nd finger on the D string.

This study combines the exercises above.

Begin with the 3rd finger on the E string.

Begin with the 3rd finger on the A string.

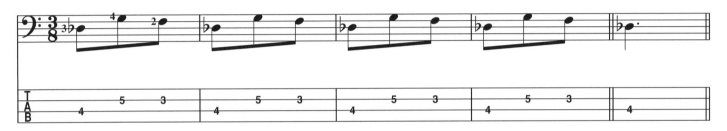

Begin with the 3rd finger on the D string.

This study combines the exercises above.

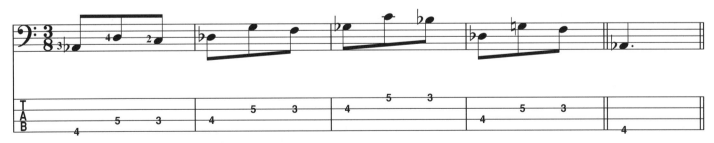

NUMBER 92

Begin with the 2nd finger on the E string.

Begin with the 2nd finger on the A string.

Begin with the 2nd finger on the D string.

This study combines the exercises above.

NUMBER 93

Begin with the 3rd finger on the E string.

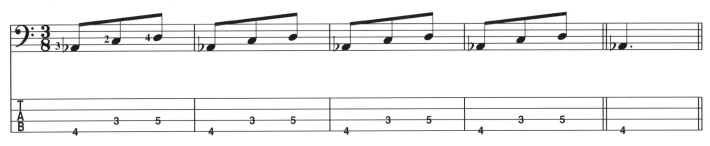

Begin with the 3rd finger on the A string.

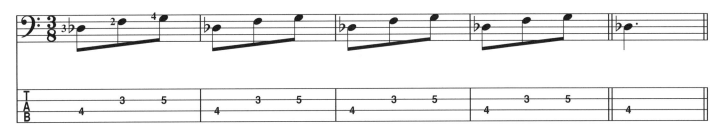

Begin with the 3rd finger on the D string.

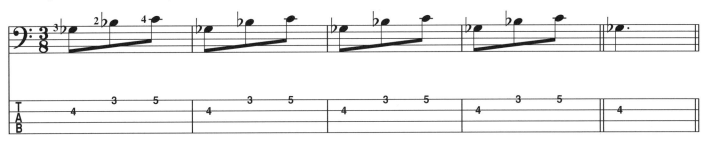

This study combines the exercises above.

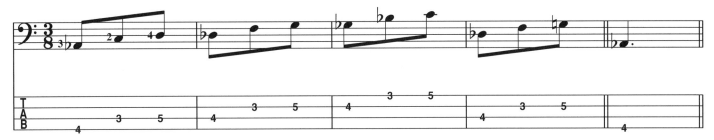

NUMBER 94

Begin with the 1st finger on the G string.

Begin with the 1st finger on the E string.

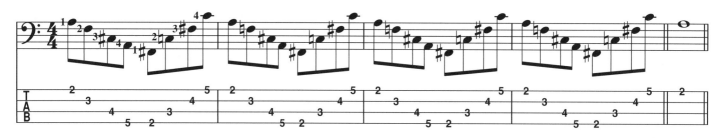

Begin with the 1st finger on the G string.

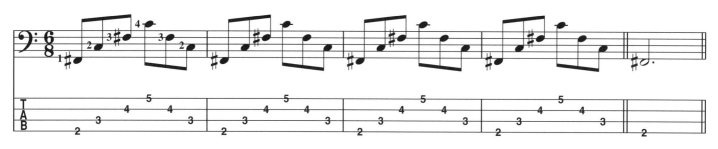

Begin with the 4th finger on the G string.

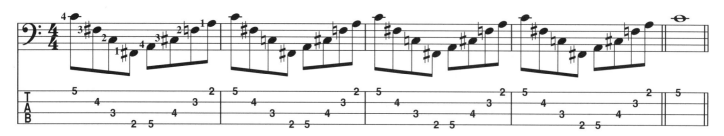

NUMBER 95

Begin with the 3rd finger on the G string.

Begin with the 3rd finger on the D string.

Begin with the 3rd finger on the A string.

This study combines the exercises above.

NUMBER 96

Begin with the 4th finger on the G string.

Begin with the 4th finger on the D string.

Begin with the 4th finger on the A string.

This study combines the exercises above.

NUMBER 97

Begin with the 2nd finger on the E string.

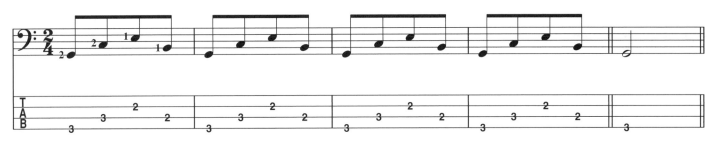

Begin with the 2nd finger on the A string.

This study combines the exercises above.

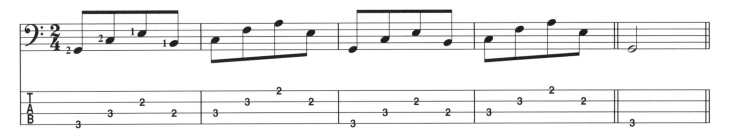

NUMBER 98

Begin with the 3rd finger on the E string.

Begin with the 3rd finger on the A string.

This study combines the exercises above.

NUMBER 99

Begin with the 4th finger on the E string.

Begin with the 4th finger on the A string.

This study combines the exercises above.

NUMBER 100

Begin with the 3rd finger on the E string.

Begin with the 3rd finger on the A string.

This study combines the exercises above.

NUMBER 101

Begin with the 4th finger on the E string.

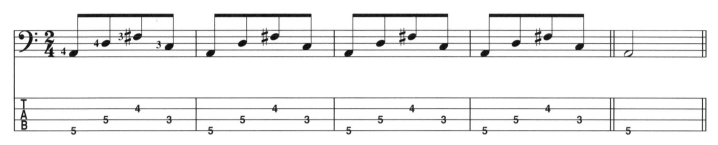

Begin with the 4th finger on the A string.

This study combines the exercises above.

NUMBER 102

Begin with the 1st finger on the D string.

Begin with the 1st finger on the A string.

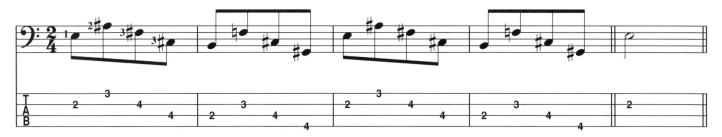

This study combines the exercises above.

NUMBER 103

Begin with the 2nd finger on the D string.

Begin with the 2nd finger on the A string.

This study combines the exercises above.

NUMBER 104

Begin with the 1st finger on the D string.

Begin with the 1st finger on the A string.

Begin with the 1st finger on the E string.

This study combines the exercises above.

NUMBER 105

Begin with the 1st finger on the D string.

Begin with the 1st finger on the A string.

Begin with the 1st finger on the E string.

This study combines the exercises above.

NUMBER 106

Begin with the 2nd finger on the D string.

Begin with the 2nd finger on the A string.

Begin with the 2nd finger on the E string.

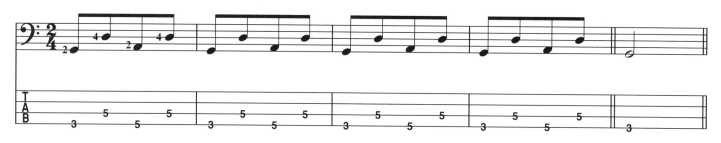

This study combines the exercises above.

NUMBER 107

Begin with the 1st finger on the E string.

Begin with the 2nd finger on the E string.

Begin with the 3rd finger on the E string.

This study combines the exercises above.

NUMBER 108

Begin with the 1st finger on the G string.

Begin with the 2nd finger on the G string.

Begin with the 3rd finger on the G string.

This study combines the exercises above.

NUMBER 109

Begin with the 1st finger on the E string.

Begin with the 2nd finger on the E string.

Begin with the 3rd finger on the E string.

Begin with the 2nd finger on the E string.

Begin with the 3rd finger on the E string.

Begin with the 4th finger on the E string.

Begin with the 2nd finger on the E string.

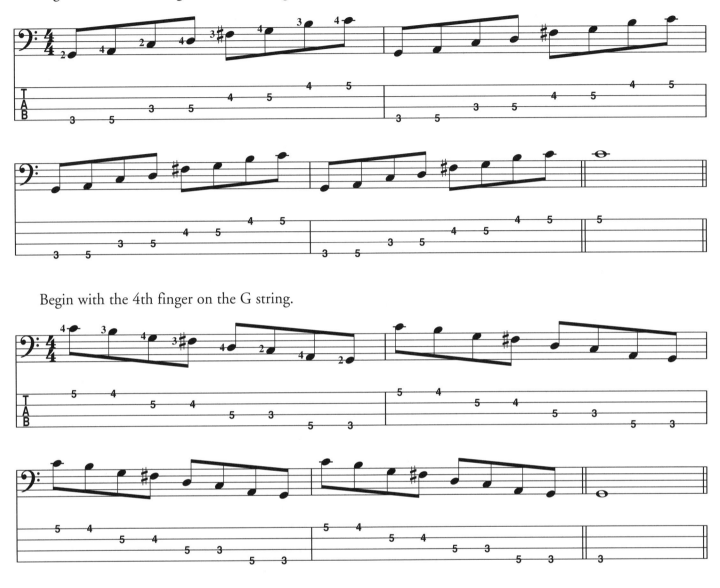

Begin with the 4th finger on the G string.

This study combines the exercises above.

Begin with the 1st finger on the E string.

Begin with the 3rd finger on the G string.

This study combines the exercises above.

NUMBER 113

Begin with the 2nd finger on the E string.

Begin with the 1st finger on the E string.

NUMBER 114

Begin with the 1st finger on the E string.

Begin with the 4th finger on the E string.

NUMBER 115

Begin with the 3rd finger on the G string.

Begin with the 3rd finger on the D string.

Begin with the 3rd finger on the A string.

Begin with the 3rd finger on the E string.

This study combines the exercises above.